This book belongs to

_____

MY BIBLE

20 *Old Testament* Bible Stories

written by
Ellen W. Caughey

illustrated by
Kathy Arbuckle

BARBOUR
PUBLISHING, INC.

Published by Barbour Publishing, Inc.
P.O. Box 719
Uhrichsville, Ohio 44683
http://www.barbourbooks.com

 Member of the
Evangelical Christian
Publishers Association

Printed in Hong Kong.

Contents

Old Testament Stories

God Makes Everything 6

One Good Man .8

A Very Tall Building 10

Can You Number the Stars? 12

No One Has a Coat Like Joseph's! 14

Moses Is the Leader 16

A City Falls Down 18

The Strongest Man 20

Ruth Meets Boaz 22

Hannah Has a Baby 24

Who Will Fight a Giant? 26

Best Friends 28

The Golden Temple 30

Elijah's God Is Your God 32

Horses of Fire .34

Jonah Learns the Hard Way 36

How Old Is King Josiah? 38

The Lions Are Hungry! 40

Esther Gives a Party 42

Nehemiah Builds a Wall 44

• • • •

The Twenty-third Psalm 46

6   *My Bible*

God Makes Everything

A long time ago God decided to make a beautiful world. Your world.

A long time ago there was only God. So only God could make everything.

In six days God made the earth and oceans, plants and trees, the sun, moon, and stars, animals, and people. On the seventh day, the day we call Sunday, God rested.

God named the first man Adam and first woman Eve. Together with all the animals, even lions and tigers, Adam and Eve lived happily in the Garden of Eden.

Remember:
God made you, too.

My Bible

One Good Man

Many years after Adam and Eve lived the world had become a scary place. Only one man listened to God. Only one man loved God. His name was Noah.

So God decided to send a big rain to wash away the earth. Only Noah and his family, and two of every animal on earth, would be saved. God would save them all in a big boat called an **ark.** Even though his neighbors laughed at him Noah kept on building the ark until it was exactly the way God wanted.

After many days of rain everyone on the ark was safe. But the earth was completely under water. Later God sent a rainbow. The rainbow was God's promise never to send such a flood again.

Remember:
God wants you to love Him.

My Bible

A Very Tall Building

Noah's family grew bigger and bigger. All the people in the world were now living near the town of Babel. They started thinking. What if they could build a building so tall it would touch the sky? Then they could rule over the rest of the world, just like God!

Blocks made from dirt were placed on top of each other. The building grew taller and taller. But God was not happy.

God wanted the people to live all over His world, not in one place. So God made the people start speaking differently. They couldn't understand each other, and they couldn't finish the building. Soon they moved away from Babel.

Remember:
God knows what is best
for you.

My Bible

Can You Number the Stars?

Not too far from Babel was the home of a man named Abraham. Like Noah, Abraham loved God, and God loved Abraham.

God told Abraham to pack everything he owned and begin a long trip. Finally, Abraham's family settled in what is now the country of Israel. God told them this would be their home forever. God also said Abraham would be the father of a people that would number more than all the stars in the sky!

How could this happen? Abraham and his wife Sarah had no children and besides, they were around 100 years old. But God always tells the truth and soon Abraham and Sarah had a little boy named Isaac.

Remember:
God always keeps His
promises.

My Bible

No One Has a Coat Like Joseph's!

Abraham's family grew and grew. Isaac had twin sons, and one of them, Jacob, had twelve sons! Jacob loved all his sons, but Joseph was his favorite. He loved him so much he gave him a coat with all the colors you can name.

Joseph's brothers were mad. They wanted to be Jacob's favorite sons, too. So they did something very bad. They sold Joseph to some men from another land, and those men took Joseph away.

But God loved Joseph. God had a plan for him. One day Joseph would be a powerful ruler in Egypt. One day Joseph and his brothers and father would be together again.

Remember:
God is always with you.

My Bible

Moses Is the Leader

Four hundred years passed and Joseph and his brothers' great-great-great-grandchildren still lived in Egypt. They were called the **Hebrews** and they were now slaves. Every day they had to work very, very hard but they still loved God.

God chose one man to lead the Hebrews back to the land of Abraham. His name was Moses.

God told Moses to talk to the king of Egypt. But the king would not let the people leave. Terrible things happened. Frogs, flies, and bugs were everywhere!

Finally the king said yes. God made a sea turn into land so the Hebrews could escape. But Moses and the Hebrews had a long way to go.

Remember:
God has something special
for you to do, too.

My Bible

A City Falls Down

As the Hebrews, now called **Israelites,** entered the land of Abraham they had a big problem. The city of Jericho with its very high walls would have to be conquered. But how?

God told Joshua, the Israelites' new leader, just how to do it. First, Joshua and the people marched in a big circle once around Jericho. Some blew on horns but no one spoke. Every day for the next six days the Israelites did this.

On the seventh day they marched seven times around the city walls and stopped. Then Joshua yelled, "Shout! The Lord has given you the city!" Suddenly, the walls of Jericho crashed down!

Remember:
God can do anything
and everything.

My Bible

The Strongest Man

Sometimes the Israelites forgot about God. Sometimes their land was taken by other peoples like the evil Philistines. You wouldn't want to meet a Philistine.

But God had not forgotten the Israelites. God chose a man named Samson to save Israel.

God had made Samson very strong. Samson was so strong he could kill a lion with his hands! But Samson had a secret: If he got a haircut his strength would be gone. One day that happened and the Philistines captured Samson. But Samson's hair grew back. At a big party Samson pulled a building down on top of thousands of Philistines.

Remember:
God will never forget you.

My Bible

Ruth Meets Boaz

Ruth and her mother-in-law Naomi were living in the town of Bethlehem. They had no husbands (they had died), no food, and no money! But things were not so bad. Ruth and Naomi loved God. They were not alone.

One of Naomi's relatives was a man named Boaz. Boaz owned what you would call a farm. When Ruth came to work in Boaz's fields something amazing happened. Boaz began to love Ruth, and Ruth began to love Boaz.

Soon they were married and later they had a son named Obed. Naomi was so proud of Obed!

Remember:
Love is a gift from God.

My Bible

Hannah Has a Baby

Hannah and her husband wanted a baby boy. So Hannah went to the temple to pray. "Please, God," she said, "if You give me a son I will give him back to You." What did that mean? Could God hear Hannah?

God gave Hannah a son named Samuel, and Hannah kept her promise to God. When Samuel was around five Hannah brought him to the temple to live with a man of God named Eli. Eli would take good care of Samuel.

But every year Hannah visited Samuel. She brought him a new coat, just like the ones Eli wore. One day Samuel would be God's **prophet.** Samuel would talk to God.

Remember:
God hears every word
you say to Him,
even if you whisper.

My Bible

Who Will Fight a Giant?

David liked to watch his sheep and play music on his harp. To keep his sheep safe David would take his slingshot and shoot stones at wild animals.

At the time there was a war in Israel. David went to see his older brothers who were fighting. The enemy had a giant named Goliath on their side. No one in Israel's army was brave enough to fight him. No one except David. With just one stone and his slingshot David killed Goliath.

Do you remember Ruth and Boaz? They were David's great-grandparents. One day David would be king of Israel.

Remember:
You don't have to be afraid
if you love God.

My Bible

Best Friends

The king of Israel was named Saul. King Saul was jealous of David. He wanted the people to like him as much as they liked David.

David knew how Saul felt so he decided to hide in a forest. While he was hiding David met Saul's son Jonathan. They promised to be best friends forever.

Later King Saul and Jonathan were killed in a war and David was finally crowned king. God loved David and while he was king Israel became very powerful. But David had not forgotten Jonathan. From then on Jonathan's son would eat at the king's table in the royal palace.

Remember:
God has promised to be
your best friend.

My Bible

The Golden Temple

When David died his son Solomon became king. One night after Solomon said his prayers he had a dream. In his dream God told him to ask for anything he wanted and his wish would be granted. Solomon gave a good answer. He asked for wisdom, that is, being able to understand great things. Solomon wanted to be a good king.

God made Solomon the smartest king who ever lived! God also let Solomon build a temple. But this was not like any other house of God. Solomon's temple was filled with gold and brass, wood cut from cedar trees, and huge stones. Seven years were spent building the temple.

Remember:
You can ask God for
wisdom, too.

My Bible

Elijah's God Is Your God

Again the Israelites forgot about God. So God sent Elijah to give a message to King Ahab.

Elijah told Ahab that there would be no rain in Israel for three years. Sure enough, not a drop of rain fell. Soon the people and animals were dying. It was time for Elijah to show the Israelites the power of God.

Elijah told Ahab to bring all his prophets to the top of a mountain. There they would have a contest. They would gather wood for two big fires, but only the one true God would light the fire. Ahab's prophets cried and sang and danced to their gods. No fire came. Then Elijah prayed, and guess what happened? Fire fell from the sky, and, in a little while, the rains came.

Remember:
There is only one God.

My Bible

Horses of Fire

With God's power Elijah brought a little boy who had died back to life. He also caused a river to dry up by throwing his robe on the water.

When Elijah's work on earth was almost finished, God told him to find a new prophet to follow him. Elijah found a man named Elisha. Elijah gave him his robe. Suddenly, a sled or **chariot** made of fire, pulled by horses also made of fire, could be seen in the sky! The chariot swooped down and picked up Elijah and carried him up to heaven.

Elisha then took Elijah's robe and threw it on the river. Once again the river dried up. Now the power of God was with Elisha.

Remember:
God wants you to have
friends who love Him, too.

My Bible

Jonah Learns the Hard Way

Do you remember the Philistines? Well, a long time later Israel had another enemy, the people of Nineveh.

God told Jonah to go to Nineveh but that was the last place Jonah wanted to go! Instead Jonah got on a ship and sailed far away. One night at sea a tremendous storm arose. The sailors were very scared. But Jonah knew the storm had come because he had disobeyed God. Jonah was right. As soon as the sailors threw him overboard, the storm stopped.

Suddenly, Jonah was swallowed whole by a great fish! Three days later the fish spit Jonah out on a beach. Later Jonah went to Nineveh and the people there began to love God.

Remember:
You can never hide
from God.

My Bible

How Old Is King Josiah?

After Ahab many kings ruled over Israel. Some were young and some were old but hardly any were as young as Josiah. He was crowned king when he was only eight years old!

When Josiah was a little older he decided to love only God and no other gods. Pretty soon everyone else in Israel loved only God, too. Josiah then ordered the temple to be made God's special house again.

Deep inside the temple some writings known as the Ten Commandments were uncovered. God had told Moses long ago to write these very words. King Josiah made all the Israelites listen to these ten best ways to live.

Remember:
God wants you to read His
Word, the Bible.

My Bible

The Lions Are Hungry!

Once the Israelites had to leave their country and live in a strange land. Daniel, an Israelite who was really God's prophet, was chosen by the king of Babylon for a special job. Sometimes he could tell the king what to do.

But some men who did not like Daniel told the king to make a new law. This law said that no one could pray to their gods. These men knew that Daniel prayed to God every day.

Daniel was thrown into a den of growling, hungry lions! But an angel of God saved Daniel and the lions did not eat him. When the king found Daniel alive the next morning, he ordered everyone to worship God.

Remember:
God loves to hear your
prayers.

Daniel 6:1-28

Esther Gives a Party

Do you like stories about kings and queens? Well, once upon a time there was a beautiful queen named Esther and she lived with her king in a big palace.

No one in the palace knew that Esther had a cousin named Mordecai. That was a good thing because one of the king's friends hated Mordecai. In fact, he wanted to kill all of Mordecai's people, the Jews!

As queen, Esther might be able to help Mordecai and save her people. She invited the king and his friend to not one but two parties where there was lots of good food. Later the king told Esther she could have anything she wanted. Esther asked that her people be saved.

Remember:
You should never hate
anyone.

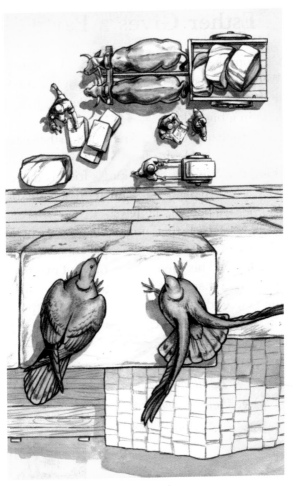

My Bible

Nehemiah Builds a Wall

Some Israelites had returned to Israel but they were in trouble. Israel's biggest city, Jerusalem, was being attacked because the city walls had fallen down.

Living in another land, a man named Nehemiah heard about the walls of his city. He decided to come home right away! Nehemiah got all the families in Jerusalem to help him rebuild the wall. Everybody worked so fast that the wall was built in fifty-two days.

Nehemiah then had the people listen to God's laws. They promised that day to love God forever. In 400 years God would send His Son to Israel. Until then no prophet would talk to God.

Remember:
God wants you
to help others.

Psalm 23

The Lord is my shepherd;
I shall not want.
He maketh me to lie down
   in green pastures:
he leadeth me beside
   the still waters.
He restoreth my soul:
he leadeth me in the paths
   of righteousness
for his name's sake.
Yea, though I walk through
   the valley of the shadow
   of death,
I will fear no evil:
for thou art with me;
thy rod and thy staff
they comfort me.
Thou preparest a table before me
in the presence of mine enemies:

thou anointest my head with oil;
my cup runneth over.
Surely goodness and mercy
shall follow me all the days
    of my life:
and I will dwell in the house
    of the Lord for ever.